tea

cookbook

tea
cookbook

Tonia George

photography by Martin Brigdale

RYLAND
PETERS
& SMALL

LONDON NEW YORK

First published in the
United States in 2008
by Ryland Peters & Small, Inc.
519 Broadway, 5th Floor
New York, NY 10012
www.rylandpeters.com

10 9 8 7 6 5 4 3 2 1

ISBN: 978 1 84597 610 1

Library of Congress Cataloging-in-
Publication Data

George, Tonia.
  Tea cookbook / Tonia George ;
photography by Martin Brigdale.
      p. cm.
  Includes index.
  ISBN 978-1-84597-610-1
  1. Cookery (Tea) 2. Tea. I. Title.
  TX817.T3G46 2008
  641.6'372--dc22

2007034247

Printed in China

Acknowledgments

Thank you to Edward Eisler of Jing Tea
for introducing me to a whole new level
of fine teas. Thanks to Martin and Helen
(and their floppy-eared doggies) for the
wonderful photography. This book is
dedicated to all my friends and family
who've inspired me along the way.

Senior Designer Amy Trombat
Editor Céline Hughes
Production Gemma Moules
Art Director Leslie Harrington
Publishing Director Alison Starling

Prop Stylist Helen Trent
Food Stylist Tonia George
Assistant Food Stylist Seiko Hatfield
Indexer Hilary Bird

Notes

• Ovens should be preheated to the
specified temperature. Recipes in this
book were tested using a regular oven.
If using a convection oven, follow the
manufacturer's instructions for adjusting
temperatures.
• All eggs are medium, unless otherwise
specified. Recipes containing raw or
partially cooked egg, or raw fish or
shellfish, should not be served to the
very young, very old, anyone with a
compromised immune system, or
pregnant women.

Making jam:
• To sterilize jam jars or bottles, wash
them in warm, soapy water and rinse in
boiling water. Put in a large saucepan,
then cover with hot water. With the lid on,
bring the water to a boil and continue
boiling for 15 minutes. Turn off the heat,
then leave the jars in the hot water until
just before they are to be filled. Invert the
jars onto clean paper towels to dry.
Sterilize the lids for 5 minutes, by boiling,
or according to the manufacturer's
instructions. Pop 2 or 3 saucers in the
fridge, ready to test for set later.
• To test for set, put ½ teaspoon of
the mixture on a chilled saucer, return
it to the fridge or freezer for about
30 seconds, or until cold, then prod
the top. If there's a skin, the jam is set.
If not, return to the pan for a little longer.

contents

tea

Cooking with tea might sound a little novel at first, but the edible leaves of the *Camellia sinensis* bush should be approached in the same way as any other dried herb. Sugar syrups infused with the perfumed leaves of jasmine, milky custards enhanced by the gentle spicing of Indian chai, and *tarte au citron* with the added fragrant earthiness of Assam all take on a special quality. You'll find that tea cookery is about delicate understatement, not provocative flavor—the flavor should tap you on the shoulder, not crash into you.

Like wine and olive oil, tea is graded according to climate, geography, the time of year it's harvested, production methods, and whether the young leaves are picked with the leaf buds. There are four main categories of tea: green, black, oolong, and white. Green tea is unfermented, keeping it fresh and grassy. The Japanese process this into Matcha powder to make green tea ice cream. Black tea, for which the leaves are rolled and then allowed to ferment, develops a more complex flavor. Oolong, known also as brown tea, is semi-fermented after the leaves have been partially withered, creating a more rounded, malty flavor. Then there's white tea (sometimes referred to as silver tip or silver needle), which uses only the dried tips of the unopened leaf bud and whose flavor has a gentle, sweet ethereal quality. Flavored teas are any type of tea blended with Indian spices, rose petals, jasmine blossoms, and essential oils, such as bergamot for Earl Grey. Herbal teas, such as Rooibos, peppermint, and chamomile, are not derived from the tea plant and as such are caffeine-free. *Tisanes* are simply herbal infusions.

As the quality, size of leaf, and strength of tea varies, when using it as a flavoring, you need to taste the infusion to check its strength. If you are going to mix it with lots of other ingredients, it needs to be powerful enough to hold its own, but not so strong that it becomes bitter. Knowing how to brew tea properly is crucial. Contrary to popular belief, tea should not always be made with boiling water. Boiling water scalds the tea, forcing out the flavor too quickly, and can make it bitter. Boiling water also de-oxygenates it—in fact, oxygen is needed to make the most of the flavor (which is why the Japanese slurp noodles and wine tasters gargle). Pay attention to your kettle: when it starts to hum and produces wisps of steam, it is probably about 160°F; once it makes popping noises and steam begins to rise vertically, it has reached 176°F. Green, oolong, delicate First Flush Darjeeling, and white teas should be made with water heated to 180°F. For all other black teas or herbal infusions, you can use water which is 196–212°F—when the steam begins to get heavier—but try to stick to the lower end of the spectrum.

Finally, if ever there was motivation to consume more tea, it is this: tea is very, very good for you. Green tea contains powerful antioxidants, which fight harmful free radicals, have cancer-fighting properties, and are good for the skin. Some studies have even shown that tea can speed up the calorie-burning process. All tea contains flavonoids, which neutralize the effect of free radicals, in turn reducing the risk of heart attacks. It also contains tannin fluoride, which helps prevent the build-up of plaque, so as long as you take your tea without sugar, it is also good for your teeth.

Here are some general tea-brewing tips:
• Use 1 heaping teaspoon tea leaves or 1 tea bag per 7 oz (¾ cup) liquid for regular-strength tea. Large leaves and teas containing flowers are less dense, so they may need 2 teaspoons per cup.
• Check the manufacturer's instructions for brewing times and quantities—they know their tea best.
• As a general rule, brew white tea for 30 seconds; green for 30–45 seconds; oolong for 1–3 minutes; black for 2–5 minutes. Strain and discard the leaves or bags so that you can reheat it later without it becoming stewed.

glossary

* **Assam** From Ceylon and India. Hearty, malty, and sometimes chocolatey or floral, with a golden red tinge.

* **Bancha** Ordinary Japanese green tea made from coarser, late-season crop.

* **Darjeeling** A region in northeast India, the Champagne of the tea world. Delicate, sharp, refreshing flavor. Muscatel Darjeeling or Second Flush varieties are even more prized for their delicate muscatel flavor.

* **Dragonwell** Sweet, fresh, and delicate Chinese green tea.

* **Earl Grey** Black tea infused with bergamot essential oil.

* **Grading system** Based on the size of processed leaves. The leaves are classified according to whether the young leaves (two, one, or none) are picked with the leaf buds. The finest quality SFTGFOP (Super Fine Tippy Golden Flowery Orange Pekoe) consists of only the leaf buds.

* **Gunpowder** Hand-rolled, pale yellow tea. Used to make Moroccan mint tea.

* **Gyokuro** Bright green, sweet, vegetally flavored high-grade tea.

* **Honeybush** Oxidized leaves from a similar plant to tea that grows wild in South Africa. Naturally sweet and mild.

* **Keemun** Chinese black tea named after the Qimen precinct of Anhui province. Sweet, toasty, and honeyed. Often used in English Breakfast with Assam.

* **Lapsang Souchong** The leaves are dried slowly over pine wood fires or burning pine oil (commercial) for a soft, lingering, smoky flavor.

* **Lemon verbena** Traditional French herbal tea, said to aid digestion.

* **Masala chai** Tea brewed in milk and spiced with pepper, cinnamon, and cardamom. Originally sold by street vendors at railway stations.

* **Matcha** Powdered green tea used in Japanese tea ceremonies, and as a food dye in baking.

* **Orange Pekoe** A variety of basic medium-grade black tea.

✳ **Peppermint** Made from dried peppermint leaves, said to aid digestion.

✳ **Rooibos (Redbush)** From the South African plant of the same name. High in antioxidants and caffeine-free.

✳ **Rosehip** A herbal tea made from dried rosehips, giving it a sour, punchy taste.

✳ **Sencha** One up from Bancha, First or Second Flush. Only the buds and baby leaves are used.

✳ **Yunnan** Named after a province of China, available as green or black, with a naturally sweet edge.

savory dishes

green tea, tofu, noodle, and cress soup

This is a fortifying soup that is really good for you: not only do you get all the benefits of green tea, but the soy proteins from the miso too. These can be destroyed by overheating, so once the miso is blended in, don't boil the soup. Green tea is best extracted at a temperature of 180°F, which is when it produces tiny bubbles.

serves 4

4 Sencha green tea bags or 1½ tablespoons Sencha green tea leaves

1¼ inches fresh ginger, peeled and thinly sliced

5 oz egg noodles

10 oz silken tofu, drained and cubed

5 oz bok choy or spring greens, shredded

1–2 tablespoons light soy sauce

2 tablespoons red or white miso paste (preferably not sweet)

½ teaspoon sesame oil

6 scallions, trimmed and sliced

½ teaspoon *nanami togarashi* (chile pepper), to garnish

a handful of *shiso* (Japanese basil) and mustard cress, to garnish

sea salt and white pepper

Put 6 cups water in a large saucepan with the green tea bags or leaves and ginger and heat until the water is about to bubble.

Meanwhile, in a separate saucepan, cook the noodles according to the manufacturer's instructions, then drain.

Remove the tea infusion from the heat and let steep for 4 minutes, then discard the tea bags or strain and discard the leaves (keep the ginger in the infusion).

Return the pan to the burner and add the tofu, bok choy, and soy sauce. Cook gently over low heat for 4 minutes. Siphon off ½ cup of the liquid and mix it with the miso paste in a small cup. Pour back into the soup, along with the sesame oil and scallions, and heat through. Season to taste with sea salt and white pepper. Divide the noodles into bowls, pour over the soup, and garnish with the *nanami togarashi*, *shiso*, and mustard cress.

mint tea couscous with roast squash, halloumi, dates, and pistachios

Peppermint tea is strong and minty, so it only needs a brief stint in hot water. It is great for fluffing up the grains of couscous and works well alongside the sweetness of squash and salty, squeaky halloumi.

serves 4–6

1 lb butternut squash or pumpkin, peeled, seeded and cut into wedges

3 tablespoons extra virgin olive oil

4 bay leaves

3 sprigs of fresh thyme

4 unpeeled garlic cloves

2 large dried chiles

8 oz halloumi cheese or *queso fresco*, cubed

3 tablespoons pistachios, shelled and chopped

2 peppermint tea bags

1¼ cups just-boiled water

1¼ cups couscous

4 oz fresh Medjool dates, pitted and finely chopped

2 tablespoons argan oil or olive oil

sea salt and freshly ground black pepper

Preheat the oven to 400°F.

Put the squash in a roasting pan, drizzle with 2 tablespoons of the olive oil, and tuck in the bay leaves, thyme, garlic cloves, and chiles. Roast in the preheated oven for 25 minutes, or until the squash is almost tender. Raise the oven temperature to 475°F. Add the halloumi or *queso fresco* and pistachios, drizzle with the remaining olive oil, and roast for a further 10 minutes for halloumi, or 7 minutes for *queso fresco*.

Meanwhile, put the peppermint tea bags in a heatproof pitcher or a teapot and pour over the hot water. Let steep for 1 minute, then discard the tea bags. Put the couscous and dates in a large bowl, season to taste, and pour over the hot tea. Cover with plastic wrap and leave for 5 minutes, or until the grains have swollen and absorbed all the tea.

Fluff up the couscous with a fork, stirring in about half the ingredients from the roasting pan at the same time, but leaving behind the whole chiles. Spoon into 4–6 bowls and top with the remaining ingredients. Drizzle with the argan oil and serve.

shrimp linguine
with fennel tea and citrus butter

Fennel has a delicate aniseed flavor that marries with the sweet flavor of plump shrimp perfectly. Citrus juice adds a little acidity, but blending orange and lemon gives it a more rounded sweetness. Just be careful not to allow the linguine to absorb all the moisture, thereby leaving the pasta dry. Keep some pasta water back— you'll need to stir in more than you think.

serves 4

3 fennel tea bags

12 oz linguine

3 tablespoons butter

2 shallots, thinly sliced

2 garlic cloves, crushed

8 oz uncooked tiger shrimp, shelled

8 scallops

freshly squeezed juice of 1 orange

freshly squeezed juice of 3 lemons

a handful of arugula

sea salt and cracked black pepper

Heat a large saucepan of water until boiling. Add 2 of the fennel tea bags, a pinch of salt, and the linguine. Cook the linguine according to the manufacturer's instructions until al dente.

Meanwhile, heat half the butter in a skillet over medium heat and cook the shallots and garlic for 2 minutes, or until soft but not colored. Add the shrimp and scallops, season to taste, and cook for 2 minutes, or until both are just cooked through. Remove from the skillet with a slotted spoon and set aside.

Add the orange and lemon juice to the skillet, open out the remaining tea bag, and scatter the contents into the juice. Bring to a boil and simmer for 2 minutes. Season to taste. Remove from the heat and beat in the remaining butter so that it becomes thick and glossy.

When the linguine is cooked, drain, reserving about ⅔ cup of its cooking water, and return to the pan it was cooked in. Add the seafood and the hot buttery sauce and toss thoroughly. If it absorbs all the liquid, gradually add the reserved pasta water until the mixture starts to look glossy and slick again. Finally, stir through the arugula and finish with plenty of cracked black pepper.

mussels in ginger and lemon tea broth

I deliberated whether this Asian-inspired version of *moules marinières* should be accompanied by a simple spiced tea broth, or a rich coconutty sauce. In the end, the coconut won. However, if you want to try a lighter and cleaner flavored broth, simply omit the coconut cream and add a splash of Chinese rice wine to the aromatics in the pan.

serves 4

3 ginger and lemon tea bags

1 cup just-boiled water

2¼ lbs live mussels, scrubbed

3 tablespoons butter

3 garlic cloves, crushed

1 lemon grass stalk (outer layer removed), finely chopped

2 red chiles, seeded and finely chopped

¼ cup coconut cream

½–1 tablespoon Thai fish sauce

a handful of Thai basil or cilantro

Put the tea bags in a heatproof pitcher or teapot and pour over the hot water. Let steep for 5 minutes, then discard the tea bags.

Meanwhile, tap the mussels against a hard surface and discard any that don't shut. Pull off any beards.

Heat half the butter in a wok or large saucepan over medium/low heat, then gently fry the garlic, lemon grass, and chiles for 1–2 minutes. Tip in the mussels and turn the heat right up. Pour in the coconut cream, ½ tablespoon fish sauce, and the tea, and cover with a tight-fitting lid. Cook for 3–4 minutes until all the mussels have opened, then stir through the basil.

Lift the mussels out of the pan with a slotted spoon and divide between 2 or 4 bowls. Taste the liquid left in the pan and add more fish sauce if you think it needs it. Spoon over the sauce (you may prefer to strain it if your mussels look like they might be gritty).

tea-smoked sea trout with beans and pancetta

Lapsang Souchong is unique among teas for its distinctive warm, smoky flavor, which makes it ideal for smoking food. Add cinnamon sticks, star anise, or any other woody herbs for a different flavor dimension. You can also try smoking shrimp, chicken breasts, and duck legs (the latter two need to be finished off in the oven).

serves 4

four 5-oz sea trout or salmon fillets, skins on, at room temperature

8 oz thin green beans, trimmed

¼ cup extra virgin olive oil

3½ oz pancetta, cubed

1½ cups cherry tomatoes, halved

a handful of fresh basil, leaves only

sea salt and freshly ground black pepper

smoking mixture

½ cup white rice

½ cup dark brown sugar

¼ cup Lapsang Souchong tea leaves

2 sprigs of fresh rosemary

4 strips of unwaxed orange peel

a large lidded wok

a wire cooling rack or trivet, to fit inside the wok

Line the inside of the wok with 3 layers of heavy aluminum foil positioned at different angles, allowing it to overhang by 2 inches. Combine all the ingredients for the smoking mixture and put them in the middle of the foil. Position the wire rack above the smoking mixture and crimp the foil around the edges to seal. Set over high heat and wait until the mixture begins to smoke. Put the trout fillets skin-side down on the rack, spaced apart. Loosely cover with 2 perpendicular layers of foil, crimping the edges to seal with the bottom layer and rack. Cook over medium heat for 8–10 minutes, depending on the size of the fillets. There should be little or no smoke escaping.

Remove the wok from the heat and keep the lid on for 5 minutes. Check that the fish is cooked by pressing the thickest part—it should flake apart easily and be opaque throughout. If not, seal it up again and cook for a little longer.

Meanwhile, bring a saucepan of salted water to a boil and cook the beans for 3–5 minutes until tender, then drain. Return the pan to the heat with the olive oil and pancetta and fry for 2–3 minutes until crisp. Add the cherry tomatoes, basil, and some seasoning. Cook for a further 2 minutes until the tomatoes soften slightly but keep their shape.

Serve the smoked trout on top of the beans, pancetta, and tomatoes.

tea and salt crusted chicken
with green herb dressing

Using a salt overcoat to keep fish beautifully moist is an age-old Mediterranean trick. Happily, it also works well with chicken, which is normally prone to dry out. The salt creates a crust which seals in the flavor and moisture, and by the end of cooking, the crust has dried out and can be removed. It isn't as salty as you might imagine and the tea flavor just adds a warm smokiness to the dish.

serves 4

4 whole chicken legs
(leg and thigh)

1 lemon, cut into 6 wedges

10 oz fava beans, shelled
and skinned

tea and salt crust

3½ lbs coarse rock sea salt

½ cup Lapsang Souchong
tea leaves

4 egg whites

green herb dressing

¼ cup extra virgin olive oil

a few grinds of black pepper

freshly squeezed juice and peel
of 1 unwaxed lemon

2 tablespoons chopped fresh
flatleaf parsley

1 tablespoon snipped fresh chives

1 tablespoon capers, rinsed

Preheat the oven to 425°F. Line a roasting pan with aluminum foil.

To make the tea and salt crust, mix the rock salt and tea leaves in a large bowl. Add half the egg whites and mix well. Gradually add the remaining egg whites until the mixture is wet enough to hold together (add a little water if necessary). Spread some of the salt mixture on the prepared roasting pan. Put the chicken legs snugly on top, pushing the lemon wedges in between. Pat the rest of the salt around the chicken in a ¼-inch thick layer. The chicken legs should be completely encased. You may need to put more on the sides where it tends to fall off. Bake in the preheated oven for 35 minutes. Let rest for 10 minutes, then break off the hardened crust and remove any stray bits of salt. Chop in half so that you end up with the leg and thigh separately.

Simmer the fava beans in boiling water for 3–4 minutes. To make the green herb dressing, heat the olive oil in a saucepan and season with black pepper. When the oil is starting to boil, remove from the heat and stir in the lemon juice and peel, parsley, chives, and capers. Serve the chicken on top of the fava beans and drizzle with the dressing.

chai-poached chicken salad with lemon and ginger dressing

Chai tea bags are a good way of flavoring a poaching liquor. If you prefer to combine your own flavors, you can use black Keemun tea with a selection of spices such as cardamom, cinnamon sticks, and star anise. The chai tints the surface of the chicken, giving it a lovely two-tone effect when you cut it. Marinating overnight keeps it moist and allows plenty of time for the flavors to be absorbed.

serves 4

¾ cup cherry tomatoes, halved

½ red onion, thinly sliced

¼ cup black olives, pitted and roughly chopped

a small handful of cilantro, leaves only

chai-poached chicken

3 chai tea bags

4 skinned chicken breasts

1 teaspoon black peppercorns

1 teaspoon sea salt

lemon and ginger dressing

1 small preserved lemon, finely chopped (about 1 tablespoon)

¼ teaspoon freshly grated ginger

1 small garlic clove, crushed

1 red chile, seeded and sliced lengthwise

½ teaspoon sugar

5 tablespoons extra virgin olive oil

To make the chai-poached chicken, put the chai tea bags in a large saucepan with the chicken breasts and 2 cups water. Bring to a boil, then reduce the heat and simmer for 5–8 minutes. Check that the thickest part of the chicken is cooked through to the center. Let cool in the tea. Cover, transfer to the fridge still submerged in the liquid, and let marinate overnight.

To make the lemon and ginger dressing, put the preserved lemon, ginger, garlic, chile, sugar, and olive oil in a screw-top jar and shake until combined. This can be made a day ahead of time, if you like.

When ready to serve, drain the chicken and cut in thick slices. Toss with the cherry tomatoes, onion, olives, cilantro, and the lemon and ginger dressing, and divide between 4 plates.

lapsang souchong pilaf with broiled quail

The Lapsang Souchong is used here to swell the grains of rice, along with a mixture of spices whose warm scents will drift through your kitchen and fill your guests with hungry anticipation.

serves 4

4 tablespoons extra virgin olive oil

2 onions, sliced

4 quail

2 teaspoons sea salt

½ teaspoon paprika

2 Lapsang Souchong tea bags or 1 tablespoon Lapsang Souchong tea leaves

1½ cups just-boiled water

3 tablespoons pine nuts

2 teaspoons ground cinnamon

1 teaspoon ground allspice

1 cup white long-grain rice

4 tomatoes, peeled, seeded, and chopped

1 tablespoon honey

6½ oz baby fava beans, shelled

3 tablespoons chopped cilantro

freshly ground black pepper

Heat 3 tablespoons of the olive oil in a large skillet and add the onions. Cover and cook over low heat for 15 minutes, stirring occasionally.

Meanwhile, put the quail breast-side down on a cutting board. Using scissors, remove the backbones and cut through the breasts so that you have 2 halves. Transfer to a shallow roasting pan and drizzle with the remaining olive oil, then season with most of the salt, some black pepper, and the paprika. Put the tea bags in a heatproof pitcher or teapot and pour over the hot water. Let steep for 3 minutes, then discard the tea bags.

When the onions are soft and beginning to turn golden, take off the lid and add the pine nuts, cinnamon, and allspice. Turn up the heat and stir-fry for 3–4 minutes until golden and caramelized. Add the rice and the remaining salt and toss to coat in the oil, then add the tomatoes and honey and simmer for 5 minutes, or until the mixture is thick. Add the fava beans and tea, then cover and cook over very low heat on the smallest ring for 12–15 minutes, or until the rice has absorbed the liquid.

Meanwhile, broil the quail under a medium-hot broiler for 8–10 minutes, or until golden, then turn them over and broil for a further 3–5 minutes.

Spoon the rice into a serving dish, and top with the quail and cilantro.

beef braised in rooibos tea with sweet potatoes

Rooibos (or Redbush) is a rich, lightly honey-flavored tea that doesn't have any bitter tannins. It is said to have tenderizing qualities too, so it works particularly well in this stew recipe. Beef brisket is ideal for pot-roasting and results in a meltingly tender texture.

serves 4–6

1¼ lbs brisket or stewing beef, trimmed of some fat and cut into 2-inch chunks

2 tablespoons flour

1 tablespoon vegetable oil

2 onions, sliced

2 celery stalks, sliced

3 garlic cloves, crushed

1 tablespoon tomato concentrate

5 Rooibos or Honeybush tea bags

1 quart just-boiled water

5 tablespoons red wine vinegar

4 strips of unwaxed orange peel

2 cinnamon sticks

2 inches fresh ginger, peeled and thickly sliced

4 small orange-fleshed sweet potatoes, peeled and thickly sliced

¾ cup honey

sea salt and freshly ground black pepper

a handful of cilantro leaves, to garnish

Season the brisket and coat in the flour. Heat the vegetable oil in a flameproof casserole dish, then add the brisket and cook over medium heat for a few minutes until golden brown all over.

Add the onions and celery and stir, then cover with a tight-fitting lid and let soften for 10 minutes. Add the garlic and tomato concentrate and cook for 1 minute.

Meanwhile, brew the tea. Put the tea bags in a large heatproof pitcher and pour over the hot water. Let steep for 4 minutes, then strain into the casserole, along with the vinegar, orange peel, cinnamon, and ginger. Turn the heat to low, cover with the lid, and cook for 2 hours, or until the meat has become quite tender. Add the sweet potatoes, honey, and plenty of seasoning and cook for a further 30 minutes, or until the potatoes are tender.

Divide between 4 plates, garnish with the cilantro, and serve.

desserts

tropical fruit salad
with jasmine tea and chile syrup

I use a very good-quality white tea with jasmine blossoms
to make this delicate fruit salad. If you feel that your tea is
not quite dewy and scented enough, you may need to add
a few more tea leaves. The chile will vary in strength too,
but make sure you use enough to be able to taste it—
it serves as a good counterbalance to the jasmine,
which would be sickly on its own.

serves 4

¾ cup just-boiled water

2 tablespoons jasmine tea leaves

6 tablespoons superfine sugar

freshly squeezed juice of 1 lime

½ red chile, seeded and shredded

20 fresh lychees, peeled,
or 6½ oz canned, drained, and
pitted lychees

1 mango, peeled, pitted, and
thinly sliced

1 papaya, peeled, seeded,
and thinly sliced

Put the hot water and tea leaves in a heatproof pitcher and let steep for
5 minutes. Strain into a saucepan and add the sugar. Cook over low
heat until the sugar has dissolved. Turn up the heat and simmer for
10 minutes until syrupy.

Stir in the lime juice and chile. Remove from the heat and let come to
room temperature.

Put the lychees, mango, and papaya in a dish and pour over the syrup.
Cover and refrigerate for 2 hours to let the fruit absorb the flavors of
the syrup.

chai custard ice cream

Masala chai, often shortened to chai, is a sweet, milky
spiced tea drink sold by street vendors all over India.
If you use shop-bought chai tea bags, you are at the mercy
of the blend, so make a cup before you start, add milk,
sweeten, and taste to see if it meets with your approval.
You can always add a little more of whatever it lacks.
Alternatively, make your own with my quantities below.

serves 4

2¾ cups whole milk

¾ cup heavy cream

1 vanilla bean, split lengthwise

5 chai tea bags (or 1 tablespoon
Keemun tea leaves, ½ teaspoon
ground cinnamon, 12 cardamom
pods, 1 tablespoon ground
allspice, and 4 fresh ginger slices)

5 egg yolks

½ cup sugar

an ice cream maker (optional)

a 4-cup freezerproof container

Pour the milk and cream into a saucepan and add the vanilla bean and
tea bags (or your chai spices). Bring to a boil over low heat—it should
take about 10 minutes. While it is cooking, squeeze the bags with the
back of a spoon to extract as much flavor as possible. When it's ready,
discard the vanilla bean and tea bags (or strain if you've used spices).

In a bowl, beat the egg yolks with the sugar. Pour the warm milk mixture
into the bowl and beat until smooth. Wash out the pan and return the
mixture to the pan. Heat the mixture over low heat, stirring regularly so
that it doesn't stick to the bottom. Heat until the custard is thick enough
to coat the back of a wooden spoon. Let cool.

When cool, strain the custard into an ice cream maker and churn
for 20 minutes until soft and velvety, then transfer to the freezerproof
container, cover, and freeze for up to 3 weeks. Remove from the freezer
and pop in the fridge 30 minutes before you are ready to serve.

If you don't have an ice cream maker, pour the cool custard directly into
the freezerproof container, cover the surface with plastic wrap, cover
with the lid, and freeze. Take out and beat with a fork every 30 minutes
to break up the ice crystals until it reaches the right consistency.

green tea panna cottas

Matcha green tea powder adds a subtle tea-like pungency to dreamy, creamy sweet panna cotta. It needs to be softly set with gelatin, but isn't tricky, and it makes the most impressive dinner party finale.

serves 4

1½ tablespoons Matcha green tea powder

6 tablespoons whole milk

2 teaspoons powdered gelatin

2 cups heavy cream

⅓ cup sugar

four 5-oz teacups or dariole molds

Gradually mix the Matcha powder with 1–2 tablespoons of the milk in a small bowl until smooth.

Pour the remaining milk into a small heatproof bowl and sprinkle over the gelatin. Set aside for about 5 minutes, then place the bowl over a shallow saucepan of hot water and stir until dissolved. Let cool.

Put the cream and sugar in a saucepan and heat over low heat until almost boiling. Remove from the heat and pour into a large glass measuring cup. Beat in the Matcha powder mixture, then the gelatin solution. Beat until fully blended. Pour the mixture into the teacups or dariole molds. Refrigerate for 1–2 hours until set. The panna cottas should wobble but they shouldn't look as though they are liquid in the center.

If you've made the panna cottas in dariole molds, dip the bases briefly in boiling water, then invert onto plates and give one short, sharp shake to loosen them. They should drop out easily. If you've made them in teacups, serve as they are.

rosehip tea and raspberry jellies with rosewater cream

Rosehip tea is not really a tea but a *tisane* or herbal infusion. There is a slightly sour edge to its floral tones, making it wonderful paired with sweetly perfumed raspberries. Get yourself a spatula and make sure every last scrap of gelatin ends up in the finished dessert, not the kitchen sink. It needs setting in two stages to keep the fruit from floating up to the top.

makes 4 jellies

1¼ cups just-boiled water

3 rosehip tea bags

1 cup plus 2 tablespoons sugar

1 tablespoon freshly squeezed lemon juice

1 tablespoon powdered gelatin

2⅓ cups raspberries

rosewater cream

¾ cup whipping cream

1–2 drops rosewater

about ⅓ cup confectioners' sugar, sifted, to taste

four tall glasses

Put the hot water and tea bags in a heatproof pitcher and let steep for 5 minutes. Discard the tea bags. Add the sugar and lemon juice and stir until the sugar has dissolved (warm it over low heat if necessary). Remove from the heat and let cool to warm room temperature.

Put ¼ cup of the tea mixture in a small heatproof bowl and sprinkle over the gelatin. Set aside for about 3 minutes, then place the bowl over a shallow saucepan of hot water and stir with a spatula until dissolved. Let cool.

Using the same spatula to scrape out every last drop, transfer the gelatin mixture to the cooled rosehip syrup, and stir gently until blended. Divide all the raspberries between the glasses and pour in enough of the jelly to almost cover the raspberries, pushing any raspberries under if necessary. Leave the remaining jelly at room temperature. Refrigerate the half-filled glasses for 30–45 minutes, or until set, then top with the remaining jelly and refrigerate for a further hour.

To make the rosewater cream, whip the cream and rosewater. Gradually add confectioners' sugar, to taste. Garnish the jellies with the cream.

deep-filled assam and lemon tart

I like my Assam tea with a slice of lemon and a little sugar, so I thought it would be fabulous to combine all three in a *pâte sucrée* pastry case. With its red hue, the Assam gives this tart a pretty russet color.

serves 6–8

pâte sucrée

5 tablespoons unsalted butter

6 tablespoons caster sugar

3 egg yolks

1⅓ cups all-purpose flour

filling

freshly squeezed juice of 4 unwaxed lemons, plus the grated peel of 2

3 tablespoons Assam tea leaves

4 whole eggs, plus 2 yolks

1 cup plus 2 tablespoons sugar

⅔ cup heavy cream

1 cup blueberries

a deep 8–9-inch loose-bottomed tart pan, lined with parchment paper

baking beans

To make the *pâte sucrée*, combine the butter, sugar, and egg yolks in a food processor. Add the flour and pulse until the mixture comes together. Wrap in plastic wrap and refrigerate for 20 minutes, or until firm.

To make the filling, put the lemon juice and tea leaves in a saucepan and heat gently until steaming. Remove from the heat and steep for 3 minutes. Strain into a bowl, pressing all the flavor from the leaves. Add the peel.

Remove the pastry from the fridge and roll out on a lightly floured surface to a 10-inch circle. Transfer to the prepared tart pan. Arrange the pastry in the bottom of the pan, so that the sides go up by at least 2¼ inches and there is a little overhang. Prick the base with a fork. Refrigerate for 15 minutes, then trim the overhang so that the sides are even.

Preheat the oven to 375°F.

Line the tart with parchment paper and fill with baking beans. Bake in the preheated oven for 15 minutes. Remove the parchment paper and baking beans and bake for a further 6 minutes, or until lightly golden and dry to the touch. Remove from the oven and reduce the temperature to 300°F. To finish the filling, beat all the eggs with the sugar, cream, and tea mixture. Pour into the pastry crust and bake for 30–35 minutes, or until it has only the merest wobble in the center. Let cool, then remove from the pan and serve with the blueberries.

pears poached in chamomile tea and spices

This is a beautiful, delicate and easy dessert. The floral notes of the chamomile with the vanilla make it a much more refined affair than that seventies classic, pears in red wine. Use firm pears, such as Bartlett, and poach them until they're soft and scoopable. The longer you cook the syrup, the stickier and more concentrated it will be—impatience sometimes gets the better of me, but I also don't like mine too thick and sickly.

serves 4–6

3 chamomile tea bags

6 cloves

4 cardamom pods

1 cinnamon stick

1 vanilla bean, split lengthwise

4 chunks of pared unwaxed lemon peel

1 cup sugar

6 small Bartlett pears, peeled

crème fraîche, to serve (optional)

Put the tea bags, cloves, cardamom, cinnamon, vanilla bean, lemon peel, and 1⅔ cups water in a deep, medium saucepan and bring to a boil. Reduce the heat, add the sugar, and heat gently until dissolved. Add the pears so that they are sitting snugly—they should be just covered with liquid. Add more water if necessary. Cover with a lid and cook over very low heat for 15–20 minutes, depending on the size of the pears.

Transfer the pears to a serving dish and cover to keep warm. Return the pan to the burner over high heat and boil the syrup vigorously for 20 minutes, or until syrupy. You should be left with a scant cup. Pour over the pears and serve with crème fraîche, if using.

sweet treats

chocolate oolong tea loaf

Milk in a chocolate cake tends to dumb down the bitter cocoa effect, so I usually prefer to add water instead, to preserve that distinctive taste. In this loaf, oolong tea is the perfect ingredient. You might think that tea is no match for chocolate in terms of strength, but what the tea adds to this cake you would miss if it weren't there—a little like vanilla essence, but instead of enhancing the sweetness, it boosts the bitterness of the chocolate.

makes 1 large loaf

⅓ cup cocoa powder

⅓ cup oolong tea, cooled

1⅓ cups all-purpose flour

2 cups plus 2 tablespoons sugar

1 teaspoon baking powder

a large pinch of salt

2 sticks (16 tablespoons) unsalted butter, softened

4 eggs, beaten

a 9 x 5 x 3-inch loaf pan, greased and lined with baking parchment

Preheat the oven to 350°F.

Mix the cocoa powder and tea together until smooth. Put the flour, sugar, baking powder, and salt in a food processor and whiz to mix. Add the butter and roughly one-third of the eggs and beat together on medium speed for 1 minute. Scrape down the batter from the sides of the food processor, add the remaining eggs and the cocoa mixture, and whiz again until smooth. Pour into the prepared loaf pan.

Bake in the preheated oven for 45–55 minutes until a skewer inserted into the center of the cake comes out clean. Remove from the oven and let cool slightly before serving.

welsh speckled tea bread

Speckled bread, or Bara Brith as it is known in Wales, is often made by plumping up the dried fruit in black tea. It is sometimes made with self-rising flour, but the traditional, yeasted version is much better. When it's a couple of days old, toast it and spread it with butter.

makes 1 loaf

⅔ cup just-boiled water

2 Darjeeling tea bags

10 oz mixed dried fruit

⅔ cup whole milk

¼ cup light muscovado sugar

1 tablespoon active dry yeast

3½ cups bread flour

1 teaspoon salt

1 teaspoon apple pie spice

1 egg, beaten

5 tablespoons unsalted butter, melted and cooled

a 9 x 5 x 3-inch loaf pan, lightly greased

Put the hot water and tea bags in a teapot and let steep for 5 minutes. Discard the tea bags. Put in a heatproof bowl with the mixed dried fruit, let cool, then cover and refrigerate overnight.

The next day, heat the milk in a small saucepan until tepid, then add 1 teaspoon of the sugar and stir until dissolved. Sprinkle over the yeast, cover, and set aside in a warm place for 10–15 minutes until frothy.

Mix the flour, the remaining sugar, the salt, and apple pie spice together in a large bowl. Make a well in the center and add the yeast mixture, egg, and butter. Mix into the dry ingredients until you have a dough that is soft but not too sticky. Knead for 10 minutes. Loosely cover with plastic wrap and set aside in a warm place for about 1½ hours until doubled in size.

Knock back the dough, then turn out onto a lightly floured surface. Flatten the dough slightly, then scatter with the drained, plumped-up dried fruit. Roll up and place seam-side down in the prepared loaf pan. Cover with plastic wrap and set aside in a warm place for a further 30–60 minutes, or until it is bursting out of its pan. Preheat the oven to 400°F.

Put the loaf in the preheated oven and reduce the heat to 350°F. Bake for 50–60 minutes. Give it a tap on the underside—it is ready when it sounds hollow. Let cool, then store in a bag for up to 4 days.

green tea cake
with green tea and lime buttercream

Matcha green tea powder is used all over Japan in baking, especially in Kyoto, and it's quite the little treasure. You buy it in a small, ornate pot and it feels very special indeed. Taste a little before you bake and you'll discover that the flavor is of a concentrated green tea: a little bitter and somewhat grassy. It also turns everything a wacky Kermit color, which I love.

serves 6–8

2½ cups all-purpose flour

1 teaspoon baking soda

1 teaspoon salt

2 tablespoons Matcha green tea powder

1⅓ cups sugar

1 cup vegetable oil

3 eggs, beaten

1 cup plain yogurt

green tea and lime buttercream

5 oz cream cheese

grated peel of 2 unwaxed limes, plus freshly squeezed juice of 1

2 tablespoons unsalted butter, softened

2 cups confectioners' sugar, plus extra to thicken

2 teaspoons Matcha green tea powder

two 8-inch round cake pans, greased and lined with baking parchment or waxed paper

Preheat the oven to 350°F.

Sift together the flour, baking soda, salt, and Matcha powder.

In a large bowl, beat together the sugar, vegetable oil, and eggs until smooth. Beat in the flour mixture alternately with the yogurt, mixing just until incorporated. Pour the batter into the prepared cake pans. Bake in the preheated oven for 30–40 minutes until a skewer inserted into the center of the cakes comes out clean. Turn out onto a wire rack and let cool for 30 minutes.

To make the green tea and lime buttercream, beat together the cream cheese, lime peel, and butter with an electric mixer until smooth. Sift in the sugar, add the Matcha powder, and beat until smooth. Add enough lime juice until you have a thick, spreadable consistency. Refrigerate for 30 minutes. Beat in a little more sugar if the mixture looks too thin.

Slice each cake in half horizontally with a serrated knife and remove the baking parchment. Place one layer on a plate and spread a little less than one-quarter of the buttercream over it. Repeat with the remaining layers and spread the remaining buttercream over the top of the cake. Refrigerate for 20 minutes to set the buttercream.

friands drenched with lemon verbena syrup

Friands are dainty little French cakes made with ground almonds, confectioners' sugar, and egg whites. They have a really light and moist consistency. With a citrusy tea syrup poured over the top, they take on a sweet, moist quality that makes them perfect for a late afternoon treat. Lemon verbena tea is delicately herbal and lemony, just as you'd expect.

makes 12 friands

6 egg whites

½ cup plus 1 tablespoon all-purpose flour

2 cups confectioners' sugar

¾ cup ground almonds

finely grated peel of 1 unwaxed lemon

12 tablespoons unsalted butter, melted and cooled

lemon verbena syrup

6 tablespoons sugar

3 tablespoons just-boiled water

2 tablespoons lemon verbena tea leaves

freshly squeezed juice of 2 lemons

a 12-hole muffin pan, greased

Preheat the oven to 400°F.

Beat the egg whites in a large, grease-free bowl until frothy. Sift the flour and confectioners' sugar over the egg whites, scatter over the ground almonds and the lemon peel, then pour in the butter. Beat the ingredients until well blended.

Pour the batter into the prepared muffin pan until the holes are about three-quarters full. Bake in the preheated oven for 20–22 minutes, or until the friands have risen and are lightly golden around the edges.

Remove from the oven and let cool in the pan for about 5 minutes. To lift them out, lay a clean kitchen towel on the kitchen counter and turn the whole pan upside down, giving them a sharp shake to release them. Transfer to a wire rack to cool.

To make the lemon verbena syrup, put the sugar, hot water, tea leaves, and lemon juice in a small saucepan and heat gently until the sugar has dissolved. Turn up the heat and simmer for a few minutes until thick and syrupy. Prick the friands 5 or 6 times with a toothpick and strain the lemon verbena syrup over them.

earl grey biscotti

Biscotti look so impressive when homemade and make gorgeous gifts stuffed into cookie jars with a pretty label. The subtle bergamot perfume of Earl Grey adds a lovely aroma. Play around by adding pecans or different dried fruit such as cranberries or cherries.

makes about 36 biscotti

2¼ cups all-purpose flour

1½ teaspoons baking powder

2 tablespoons Earl Grey tea leaves

½ teaspoon salt

1 stick (8 tablespoons) unsalted butter, softened and cubed

¾ cup sugar

2 eggs, beaten

2 tablespoons whole milk

3 tablespoons blanched almonds, roughly chopped

3½ oz dried apricots, roughly chopped

Preheat the oven to 350°F.

Put the flour, baking powder, tea leaves, and salt in a food processor and pulse until the tea leaves are finely ground. Alternatively, grind the tea leaves in a clean coffee grinder, then combine with the flour, baking powder, and salt in a bowl. Add the butter and sugar and pulse or mix with your fingertips until the mixture resembles bread crumbs.

Pour in the eggs and milk and pulse or mix until the dough comes together. Take out and knead in the almonds and apricots. Divide the dough in half and shape into 2 flat logs, about 10 x 2 inches. Space them apart on a baking sheet and bake in the preheated oven for 20 minutes, or until golden.

Remove from the oven and let cool for about 5 minutes. Using a serrated knife, cut into ½-inch thick slices while the biscotti are still warm and arrange cut-side up on 2 baking sheets. Bake for a further 12–15 minutes, or until the edges become tinged with brown and crisp up. Remove from the oven and let cool on wire racks. Store for up to 7 days in an airtight container. Serve with a cup of Earl Grey tea.

peppermint tea and apple jelly

This is a great jelly for eating with roast lamb. You could also add some chopped garden mint once the whole thing is cooked before transferring into jars.

makes 4 jars

6 peppermint tea bags

5 lbs cooking apples, unpeeled, washed, and roughly chopped

6 tablespoons cider vinegar

5 cups jam sugar

four sterilized 8-oz jam jars (page 4) with screw bands and new lids

a jelly bag or cheesecloth

a baking pan, lined with parchment paper

Put 1 quart water in a large preserving pan or non-aluminum saucepan and bring to a boil. Add the tea bags, remove from the heat, and let steep for 5 minutes. Discard the tea bags.

Add the apples (cores and peel included) to the pan and cover with a lid. Cook gently over low heat for about 1 hour until very tender and collapsed. Add the vinegar and remove from the heat. Sterilize the jelly bag by running it through boiling water, then hang from a handle of a wall unit and put a large, sterilized bowl underneath it. Transfer the apple pulp to the bag and leave for 30 minutes, or until it stops dripping.

Preheat the oven to 325°F. Put the jam sugar in the prepared baking pan and pop it in the oven for 5 minutes to warm through.

Measure the juice you have collected (you should have about 7 cups) and add the warmed sugar. If your yield of juice is different, adjust the amount of sugar to the ratio of a scant cup sugar to 1 cup clear juice. Return the mixture to a pan over low heat and let the sugar dissolve slowly. Stir occasionally. Once the sugar has dissolved, turn up the heat and boil for 15 minutes, or until setting point is reached (a sugar thermometer should read 220°F). Test for set (page 4). Ladle the hot jelly into the jars, leaving ¼-inch headroom. Take care of any smudges with a paper towel. Put the lids on top and screw down the bands tightly. Store in a cool, dark place for up to 6 months.

white tea and apricot jam

Use apricots that are firm and unripe for this jam because the pectin levels are higher at this stage. White tea has a naturally peachy aroma, so it adds a lovely fragrant undertone here. Adding the apricot kernels is a good trick too and worth doing for the nutty perfume they exude.

makes 5 jars

2 tablespoons silver tip white tea leaves or 3 silver tip white tea bags

1 cup just-boiled water

1½ lbs (about 15) fresh apricots

freshly squeezed juice of ½ lemon

3¾ cups jam sugar

five sterilized 8-oz jam jars (page 4) with screw bands and new lids

a baking pan, lined with parchment paper

Put the tea leaves and hot water in a teapot and let steep for 3–4 minutes.

Halve the apricots and remove the pits. Pop the pits in a plastic freezer bag and whack with a rolling pin so the pits break and release the kernels. You only need 5–6 kernels so discard the rest.

Strain the white tea into a large preserving pan or non-aluminum saucepan, add the apricots, kernels, and lemon juice and bring to a boil. Cook the apricots for 20 minutes, or until they collapse. You can squash them with the back of your spoon to help break up any large pieces of fruit.

Preheat the oven to 325°F. Put the jam sugar in the prepared baking pan and pop it in the oven for 5 minutes to warm through.

Pour the warmed sugar into the pan with the apricots and cook over low heat until the sugar has dissolved. Once the sugar has dissolved, turn up the heat and boil for about 15 minutes, or until setting point is reached (a sugar thermometer should read 220°F). Test for set (page 4). Ladle the hot jam into the jars, leaving ¼-inch headroom. Take care of any smudges with a paper towel. Put the lids on and screw down the bands tightly. Store in a cool, dark place for up to 6 months.

earl grey chocolate truffles

Use salted butter here as it cuts through the richness of the truffles. The Earl Grey can be strong and overpowering, so keep it to a minimum to begin with.

makes about 36 truffles

1¼ cups heavy cream, plus extra if necessary

5 tablespoons Earl Grey tea leaves

8 oz bittersweet chocolate, roughly chopped

2 tablespoons salted butter

1 tablespoon cocoa powder

*an 8-inch square cake pan,
lined with baking parchment*

Put the cream and tea leaves in a small saucepan and bring to a boil. Remove from the heat and let steep for 15 minutes. Strain into a small bowl, making sure you press all the flavor from the leaves and top up to 1 cup cream if the tea leaves have absorbed lots of the liquid.

Put the chocolate and butter in a heatproof bowl over a saucepan of barely simmering water. Make sure the bowl does not touch the water. Stir until thoroughly melted, then remove from the heat. Pour the infused cream into the chocolate mixture and stir until velvety smooth. Pour into the prepared cake pan—it should be about 1 inch deep. Refrigerate for 2 hours, or until firm.

Tip out onto a cutting board and cut into 1¼-inch squares. Sift over the cocoa powder. Store in the fridge and eat within 3 days.

peppermint tea and chocolate crunches

These are truffles with a difference—they have crispy, crunchy bits in them. They're very easy to make and a perfect gift for a chocoholic friend.

makes 48 crunches

⅔ cup heavy cream

3 peppermint tea bags

8 oz bittersweet chocolate, finely chopped

3 tablespoons demerara sugar

*an 8 x 12-inch baking sheet,
lined with baking parchment*

Put the cream and tea bags in a small saucepan and bring to a boil. Remove from the heat and let steep for 5 minutes. Strain into a heatproof bowl, making sure you press all the flavor from the tea bags. Add the chocolate and set over a saucepan of barely simmering water. Make sure the bowl does not touch the water. Stir until velvety smooth, then remove from the heat.

Let cool, then stir in the sugar. You need this to provide the crunch, so make sure the mixture is too cool for the sugar to dissolve. Pour the chocolate on the prepared baking sheet and spread it out, with a spatula, to ¼ inch thick. Refrigerate for 1 hour, or until firm.

Tip out onto a cutting board and cut into 2-inch squares, then into triangles. Peel off the baking parchment. Store in the fridge and eat within 3 days.

drinks

chai vanilla milk shake

The flavors of chai are wonderful combined with vanilla ice cream to make an unctuous milk shake. I sometimes add a ripe banana too, but this version is just as good.

makes 4 milk shakes

1 quart whole milk

6 tablespoons light brown sugar

2 tablespoons black tea leaves

1 vanilla bean, split lengthwise

¼ teaspoon ground cinnamon

8 cardamom pods

¼ teaspoon ground allspice

3 scoops of vanilla ice cream

ice cube trays

Put 3¼ cups of the milk, the sugar, tea leaves, vanilla bean, cinnamon, cardamom, and allspice in a saucepan and bring to a boil. Reduce the heat and simmer gently for 5 minutes, then turn off the heat, cover, and leave for 10 minutes. Strain into the ice cube trays and freeze until solid. Freeze 4 tall glasses.

When ready to serve, pop the frozen chai cubes in a blender with the remaining milk and the ice cream and blend until smooth.

moroccan fresh mint tea

Taking a glass of mint tea is an important ritual in North Africa and it is thought rude if you drink any less than two cups. The Chinese green tea used for this popular drink is Gunpowder tea, which is crisp and fresh. The tea is rolled into a small pellet, which most probably accounts for the name. However, I like the fact that "freshly brewed" in Mandarin is *gang paò dè*, which bears more than a striking resemblance to the word.

serves 2

2 tablespoons Chinese Gunpowder green tea leaves or 3 green tea bags

a handful of fresh mint leaves

6 tablespoons superfine sugar

sugar cubes, to serve

Put the tea leaves in a warmed teapot with two-thirds of the mint leaves and and all the sugar. Heat 2½ cups water to 180°F, just before the water starts to bubble, and pour into the teapot. Let steep for 6 minutes. Put the remaining mint in 2 heatproof glasses. Strain the tea into the glasses and serve with sugar cubes.

iced peach and elderflower tea

Make a pitcher of this on weekends and keep it in the fridge for slurping throughout the day. The tea you use should have some bitterness and tannins to contrast against the sweetness of both the elderflower and peach juice.

serves 6–8

6 black tea bags, such as Keemun or English Breakfast

7 cups just-boiled water

6 tablespoons elderflower cordial

1 cup peach juice

peach slices and raspberries, to serve

ice cubes, to serve

Put the tea bags in a large heatproof pitcher or bowl and pour over the hot water. Let steep for 3–4 minutes, then remove the tea bags and let cool until lukewarm. Add the elderflower cordial and peach juice and give it a good stir. Leave until cold, then add the peach slices, raspberries, and ice cubes to serve.

hot tea toddy

A cure-all for colds as well as a good night-time drink to help you sleep. Try to use a subtle whisky, such as Scotch or a single malt, not bourbon or Tennessee whiskey, which are too strongly flavored. The amount of lemon and honey is down to personal preference, so taste as you go.

makes 2 toddies

2 lemons, plus extra juice to taste

6 cloves

2 chamomile tea bags or
1 tablespoon chamomile tea leaves

1⅔ cups just-boiled water

2 cinnamon sticks

a pinch of freshly grated nutmeg

1–3 tablespoons honey,
plus extra to taste

3 oz whisky

Cut half a lemon into slices and stud the skin of each slice with the cloves. Put the tea bags, hot water, cinnamon, nutmeg, and lemon slices in a saucepan and simmer for 2–3 minutes.

Meanwhile, squeeze the juice from the remaining lemons. Take the tea mixture off the heat and add the lemon juice, honey, and whisky. Taste and add more lemon or honey if necessary.

Strain the tea into 2 heatproof glasses or mugs and drop a lemon slice and cinnamon stick into each glass. Give it one final stir with the cinnamon stick before drinking.

green tea martini

serves 2

1 tablespoon superfine sugar

½ cup hot green tea

2 oz citron vodka

2 teaspoons Cointreau

ice cubes

an orange twist

a cocktail shaker

Put the sugar in the hot green tea and stir until it has dissolved. Let cool. Put in the cocktail shaker with the vodka, Cointreau, and some ice cubes. Shake well and strain into 2 Martini glasses. Garnish with an orange twist.

g & tea

serves 1

2 tablespoons superfine sugar

3 tablespoons hot black tea

3 tablespoons gin

freshly squeezed juice of ½ lemon, plus 1 lemon wedge, to serve

ice cubes

¾ cup tonic water

Put the sugar in the hot black tea and stir until it has dissolved. Let cool. Add the gin and lemon juice and stir. Fill a highball glass with some ice cubes, pour over the tea mixture, and top with the tonic water. Garnish with the lemon wedge.

blackberry tea vodka

makes 2 bottles

36 oz vodka

4 blackberry tea bags

1½ cups superfine sugar

1 lb blackberries, plus extra to serve

ice cubes or soda water, to serve

two sterilized 3-cup bottles or containers (page 4)

Put 4 oz of the vodka in a bowl and drop in the tea bags. Cover and let steep overnight. Divide the tea mixture between the sterilized bottles. Put half the remaining vodka, sugar, and blackberries in each bottle. Cover and refrigerate, shaking each day to dissolve the sugar and mix the flavors. After about a month, strain through a fine-mesh sieve, discard the berries, and rebottle. Serve on ice or with soda water, with extra blackberries.

index

conversion chart

Weights and measures have been rounded u
or down slightly to make measuring easier.

Measuring butter:
A US stick of butter weighs 4 oz which is
approximately 115 g or 8 tablespoons.

The recipes in this book require the
following conversions:

American	Metric	Imperial
6 tbsp	85 g	3 oz
7 tbsp	100 g	3½ oz
1 stick	115 g	4 oz

Volume equivalents:

American	Metric	Imperial
1 teaspoon	5 ml	
1 tablespoon	15 ml	
¼ cup	60 ml	2 fl oz
⅓ cup	75 ml	2½ fl oz
½ cup	125 ml	4 fl oz
⅔ cup	150 ml	5 fl oz (¼ pint)
¾ cup	175 ml	6 fl oz
1 cup	250 ml	8 fl oz

Weight equivalents: **Measurements:**

Imperial	Metric	Inches	cm
1 oz	30 g	¼ inch	5 mr
2 oz	55 g	½ inch	1 cm
3 oz	85 g	1 inch	2.5 cr
3½ oz	100 g	2 inches	5 cm
4 oz	115 g	3 inches	7 cm
6 oz	175 g	4 inches	10 cm
8 oz (½ lb)	225 g	5 inches	12 cm
9 oz	250 g	6 inches	15 cm
10 oz	280 g	7 inches	18 cm
12 oz	350 g	8 inches	20 cm
13 oz	375 g	9 inches	23 cm
14 oz	400 g	10 inches	25 cm
15 oz	425 g	11 inches	28 cm
16 oz (1 lb)	450 g	12 inches	30 cm

Oven temperatures:

120°C	(250°F)	Gas ½
140°C	(275°F)	Gas 1
150°C	(300°F)	Gas 2
170°C	(325°F)	Gas 3
180°C	(350°F)	Gas 4
190°C	(375°F)	Gas 5
200°C	(400°F)	Gas 6
220°C	(425°F)	Gas 7

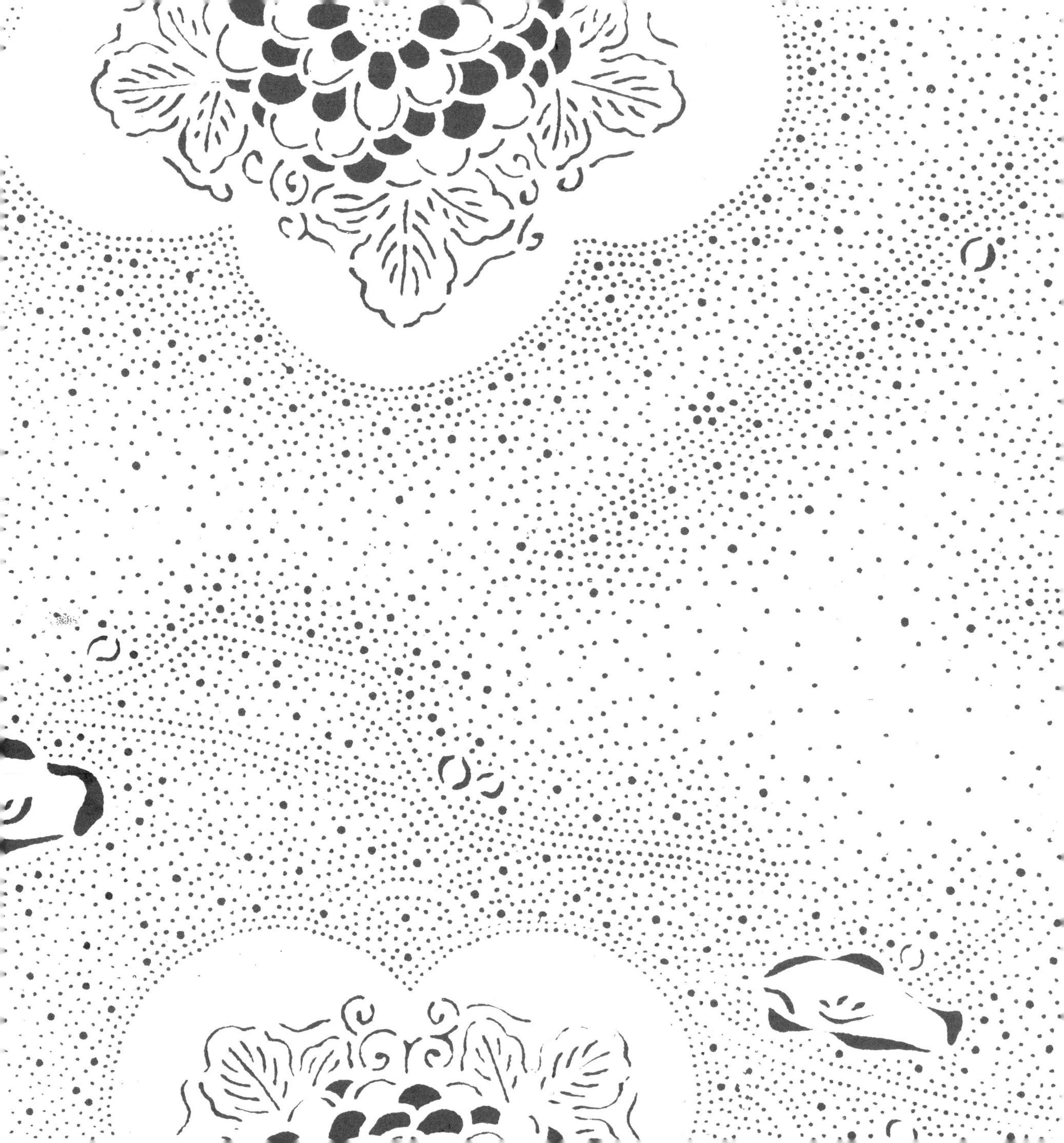